D0254855

Contents

Acknowledgments   ix
Introduction   xi

1. The Order—Not Just a Grocery List   1
2. The Gathering   5
3. Addressed by the Word   10
4. The Joyful Feast   16
5. Sent to Serve   21
6. Music and the Arts in Worship   25
7. Worship for Special Times   33
8. Celebrating Christmas (and Epiphany)   37
9. Advent as Preparation   42
10. Celebrating Easter   46
11. Lent and Holy Week: Journeying with Christ   53
12. The Great Fifty Days of Easter and
    Pentecost Day—Celebration Overflowing   57
13. Liturgical Odds and Ends: Meaningful
    Moments and Conversations   60
14. Is Worship Important?   66

Notes   71
Bibliography   75

Rhythms of Worship

Rhythms of Worship

The Planning and Purpose of Liturgy

John G. Stevens
and Michael Waschevski

WJK WESTMINSTER
JOHN KNOX PRESS
LOUISVILLE • KENTUCKY

© 2014 John G. Stevens and Michael Waschevski

First edition
Published by Westminster John Knox Press
Louisville, Kentucky

14 15 16 17 18 19 20 21 22 23—10 9 8 7 6 5 4 3 2 1

Book design by Sharon Adams
Cover design by Dilu Nicholas
Cover illustration: Abstract music volume equalizer infinity computer technology
© vs148/www.shutterstock.com

Library of Congress Cataloging-in-Publication Data

Stevens, John G.
  Rhythms of worship : the planning and purpose of liturgy / John G. Stevens and Michael Waschevski. -- First edition.
      pages cm
  Includes bibliographical references.
  ISBN 978-0-664-26017-0 (alk. paper)
  1. Worship. 2. Worship--Planning. 3. Liturgics. I. Title.
  BV15.S695 2014
  264--dc23
                                                              2014029381

♾ The paper used in this publication meets the minimum requirements of the American National Standard for Information Sciences—Permanence of Paper for Printed Library Materials, ANSI Z39.48-1992.

Most Westminster John Knox Press books are available at special quantity discounts when purchased in bulk by corporations, organizations, and special-interest groups. For more information, please e-mail SpecialSales@wjkbooks.com.

We dedicate this book to the congregations we have worshiped
with and served over the years, especially our current congregations
of Westminster Presbyterian Church in Sacramento, California,
and First Presbyterian Church in Fort Worth, Texas.
They inspire, nurture, and deepen our faith in so many ways.
We are grateful for their faithful worship and witness.

130190

Acknowledgments

First, we want to thank Sharyl Stevens, John's wife and Michael's mother. Not only has she supported and encouraged us in this project (and in life), but she is an astute lay liturgical theologian herself. We are grateful not only for her tireless proofreading but also for her substantive suggestions and responses to the early editions of the text. They have been invaluable. Plus, and most importantly, we love her!

Second, we also thank our editor, David Maxwell of Westminster John Knox Press, for his support and encouragement, which began when he first read the manuscript in rough form and saw the project through to publication. We have greatly appreciated and benefited from his guidance and advice.

Finally, thank you to our colleagues, mentors, and partners in worship leadership over the years. We wish we could name and thank each one of you! A special thank you from Michael to the Rev. Karl Travis, the Rev. Robyn Michalove, and the Rev. Joshua Stewart. You are not only outstanding clergy colleagues with whom I am privileged to lead worship on a regular basis, you are dear friends. John extends his special thanks to Dr. Arlo D. Duba, who guided him through a doctoral dissertation and project focused on worship, baptism, and Easter; to the Rev. Robert H. Fernandez, who read the early manuscript and made many helpful suggestions; and to the Rev. Wes Nordman, pastor at Westminster Presbyterian Church in Sacramento, California, who saw the potential value of such a book and was enthusiastic and supportive.

Introduction

When worship works, in us and among us, we know it. Something connects. Something speaks powerfully within us. A divine contact is made at the center of our lives. Diverse things link up for us. We are stirred, perhaps moved to tears or filled with joy. We are motivated to action. We want to talk about it and to share what has touched us deeply.

Of course, that doesn't always happen. It doesn't happen just because we want it to or just because we call it worship. The day of worship arrives, the doors are opened, and the lights are on. There is music. People assemble. Someone reads. Someone addresses the gathering. Everything seems to be in place, but somehow it doesn't work. It falls flat. It leaves us empty. We may have no idea why.

The difference between worship that works and worship that somehow doesn't work is never totally under our control. Spirit blows where Spirit wills! The serendipitous is not subject to our control. But there are things we can control, and plan, and manage—and we should. It only makes sense to give to the Spirit the best preparation and creativity we have to offer.

Congregations have much at stake in planning and providing excellent worship. Such worship is key for a spiritually alive and healthy congregation and for each member's spiritual growth and effectiveness as a contemporary disciple of Jesus Christ. The more that leaders and members of a congregation share a basic perspective concerning the elements and dynamics of Christian worship, the more likely it is that a congregation will benefit from collaborative worship planning and deeply satisfying participation.

For such worship planning to be effective, a shared perspective on the meaning of worship is helpful, if not essential. Each person involved in helping to plan a congregation's worship will bring his or her own perspectives, drawn from many sources and personal experiences. Our hope is that this resource will help to provide planners with a *shared* basic theology of Christian worship and a sense of the meaning of what happens in all the parts of worship on a Sunday morning and throughout the seasons of the Christian year.

This book is for *congregations*. There are many books available for liturgical experts, but there continues to be a huge gap between those who are comfortable talking scholarly language and most members of most congregations. This book aims to help bridge that gap in order to develop a shared understanding among pastoral leaders, musicians, worship committee members, and all who make their way to church each Lord's Day to worship God.

Our aim is to describe in clear everyday language why we worship as we do and to help equip worship planners and leaders for excellence in their ministry. The sequence of each movement within a typical Lord's Day service is explained in terms of how it expresses our Christ-centered faith. The feasts and festivals of the liturgical year are described in clear language and with an eye to understanding what they mean and how they contribute to the enrichment and development of our faith. There is also a full chapter on music for worship, singing in an expanded variety of genres and styles, the use of technology, and the use of other art forms in the liturgy. The book closes with a strong affirmation of worship in the life of the church and for our faith as disciples of Jesus Christ.

We hope that as you read and discuss these chapters you will find them clear and practical. Rather than trying to be exhaustive in scope and detail, we have tried to paint the big picture, to describe the flow and direction of congregational worship, and to suggest ways of enhancing its rhythms and dynamics. Questions at the conclusion of each chapter are for use with small groups, worship committees, and worship planners as they engage you in conversation. We look forward to being in "conversation" with you as you seek to offer worship that inspires and equips your congregations for faithful discipleship.

John G. Stevens
Michael Waschevski

Chapter One

The Order—Not Just a Grocery List

Take a look at your congregation's worship bulletin. It is a description of what typically happens in your service of worship. First there is this, and then there is that. You begin at the top, and when you get to the bottom you are done. After socializing a bit, you can go home. Simple enough.

But worship is not just a random "grocery list" of things to do when we gather together. There is a dynamic, a flow, a sequence that makes worship meaningful and satisfying. There is a beginning, a middle, and an end. One action prepares for another, and that action flows into the next. When things are out of sequence, you sense that something is wrong. This isn't just a matter of what you are used to. Something that is just stuck in somewhere is likely to violate the logic of worship. It will feel stuck in.

We are speaking here of the *order* of worship.[1] The order makes sense. It follows an understandable sequence. It is similar to the order that is involved in going to dinner at the home of friends. You arrive at their house, go to the door, and ring the bell. The door opens, and there is a ritual of welcome, which continues as you enter their house and exchange comments and greetings that express the joy of being together and of sharing time with one another. This is followed by a time of conversation and visiting. Then you gather at the table and share the meal, enjoying the food and the company—an informal ritual celebrating the joy of life. Later there is a final ritual of departure at the door in which you express thanks and good wishes as you leave to go home. It just doesn't make sense to reverse or mix up anything in this familiar sequence.

In the same way, there is a pattern of worship that reflects the church's long history and tradition, a four-fold pattern that remains common within most mainline denominations:

1. Gathering in response to the love and invitation of God
2. Hearing and responding to God's Word
3. Sharing the meal and giving thanks
4. Departing to serve God in the world

This common pattern is remarkably similar to the pattern of having dinner with friends. It too is a sequence that makes sense.

There is no need to start from scratch in order to establish the basic shape of a congregation's worship. It does not need to be reinvented. It is a part of our heritage. Beyond this basic shape, or order, a congregation should give careful attention to its own denominational standards. There is just too much accumulated wisdom and experience in our denominational traditions to ignore.

Look again at your worship bulletin. In addition to

major headings that reflect the fourfold structure of Christian worship and headings that indicate the specific actions within each of those sections, does the bulletin provide texts and tunes and actions to facilitate congregational participation? If the answer to this question is no, then your service has the character of a monologue. With the exception of the songs and hymns sung by the congregation and perhaps music provided by a choir or soloist, the only voice that is heard is the voice from the front, usually the voice of the pastor or worship leader. The congregation's role is limited, passive, and submissive. But if the answer is yes, there is an expectation that the congregation is to participate actively in the service of worship. Every opportunity for the congregation to speak or sing or act in some particular way is in fact a kind of symbol that the people who have assembled for worship are invited and expected to participate actively (and probably not just in worship but also in the life of the congregation and in its witness and service to the world).

In this section, we have identified two important aspects of Christian worship. The first is its historic fourfold order, its overall sequence. The second is its interactive, responsive, participatory character. Both are crucial if the congregational worship we experience is to be as spiritually powerful and effective as it can be.

Worship forms us to live as disciples of Jesus Christ, here and now. In worship, God calls us into a disciple-forming dialogue, a living and continuing conversation. In worship we experience God's welcome, grace, and love. In worship we are addressed, nurtured, equipped, and motivated to be God's people, living our lives as part of God's reign of love for all people and for the whole creation. Worship is not a time of escape from our real lives. It is not a fantasy journey into the long ago and far away. It is always a matter of what is happening now.

In the chapters that follow, we will consider what happens in each of the four major movements of a service of worship, looking at the content and dynamics of each segment. The purpose is to give a sense of the feel and function of each segment of the service of worship, and how it prepares for and flows into the next segment.

Questions for Reflection

1. What elements of the worship service are most engaging for you? Why?
2. Gather several weeks of your congregation's worship bulletins. Do you find the order of worship fairly consistent or quite varied? Does your order of worship make sense to you? Why or why not?
3. Do you find major movements in your service of worship? Are they identified by understandable headings? How do they help identify where the service is going?

Chapter Two

The Gathering

Worship begins with gathering. That may sound overly simplistic, but it is actually very significant. Gordon W. Lathrop, a renowned Lutheran liturgical theologian, says simply, "The Church is an assembly of people. In order to have 'church' a group of people must first gather."[1]

The elements that compose the gathering liturgy help us to move from our everyday activities and relationships into a time of gathering with others and centering on God's presence and purpose. This transition actually begins before our arrival at the place of worship and well before the worship service itself begins. It includes washing and dressing, leaving home, traveling to the place of worship, greeting others who have assembled, and then settling into one's pew or chair. Time has to be allowed for all these things to happen, even more so if one also has responsibilities such as serving as a greeter or an usher or singing in the choir.

The time for greeting that takes place before the service of worship begins is very important, and sufficient time should be allowed for it. Significant words are often exchanged during this time. Important information is shared. Support and encouragement are expressed. All these things, and more, are part of the formation of the community that has come together for worship. There may be some for whom the greeting time provides their one meaningful human contact for the week.

It is important that worship begin reliably on time. This means that one's expected time of arrival should be comfortably earlier than the start of the service. Such an expectation can be an important part of a congregation's worship education. This is not to make a fetish out of watching the clock. It is, rather, to encourage the members of the congregation to allow themselves sufficient time for their transition into worship before the service begins.

When the hour of worship arrives, a worship leader might welcome the congregation and share any information the congregation might need in order to participate meaningfully in the service. The leader might then say something like "Now let us prepare our hearts and minds to worship God together." A musical prelude would naturally follow.

Or perhaps a short prelude might begin the service, with a note in the worship bulletin helping the congregation make good use of the prelude in preparation for the service. (For example: "Please use the prelude to make the transition from getting here to being here. Open yourself to the Spirit of God moving in our midst.") The prelude might then be followed by a brief welcome from a worship leader and the sharing of any information the congregation would need in order to participate meaningfully in the service. Other announcements are best kept to a minimum so as not to derail the energy and the expectation that worship has begun.

Printed announcements in the bulletin or in a hand-out are effective ways of minimizing verbal announcements that do not pertain directly to the worship service itself. Opportunities and invitations for participation in the mission and ministry of the congregation make more sense later in the service as a response to the Word read and proclaimed.

The liturgy of gathering is and should be short and joyous, an affirmation of the gracious invitation of God. The call to worship proclaims the good news of God's forgiving love for us and for all people. Selected verses of Scripture (often from Psalms or the Epistles) provide rich resources for the call to worship. The gracious invitation comes from God; praise and gratitude is our response. Therefore, the tone and mood that begin our worship should not be weak, apologetic, or tentative. God's gracious love is the best news in the world!

The call to worship may be followed by a prayer of thanksgiving and a hymn, or a sung psalm, or another appropriate song of praise to God. Recalling and proclaiming the grace and goodness of God, our praise can then lead into confession and pardon. Because God's loving grace is prior to our confession, we are freed from our defenses and can place ourselves in God's holy presence with confidence—and without pretense. We have a history, we are just what we are, we are fallible, we are self-centered, and we are subject to the compromises and sins to which human life is prone. Yet God loves us still! We don't need to wallow in our sense of sinfulness. We can simply come clean, be honest with God, and admit that as individuals and as members of families and communities and, indeed, as part of the church, we share the human condition and stand in need of God's redeeming love and pardon.

Confession is followed immediately by the assurance of God's pardon. Pardoned and reconciled with God, we are invited to be reconciled to one another. This movement of reconciliation—from Christ to us, and from each of us to those around us, and from all of us to the world—is often expressed in a liturgical action called the exchange of peace or the passing of the peace. It is *the peace of Christ* we are exchanging, not family news or a new recipe. This is not a coffee break in the midst of worship, but rather a significant theological and religious moment. We simply reach out to those around us in worship and say to them, "The peace of Christ be with you," with the response, "And also with you." We may also use other words appropriate to the message of forgiveness and reconciliation.

The liturgy of gathering may then appropriately conclude with the Gloria Patri,[2] the Gloria in Excelsis,[3] or other musical praises to God. In this way our sin, our confession, all our difficulties in all our relationships, and our prayers for pardon for all that is negative in our lives and in the church are taken up into God's great love and grace given to us in Jesus Christ. We are now ready to turn away from our self-concern and to hear the word that God addresses to us today.

Questions for Reflection

1. What is your response to the suggestion that preparation for worship can begin even before one leaves home? How might we prepare ourselves to worship with God in mind?

2. What could be done to encourage folks to arrive early enough to greet others before the announced hour of worship?

3. If your liturgy does not follow the sequence outlined (call to worship, confession, reconciliation expressed in the passing of the peace), how does your opening sequence flow? What purpose(s) does it accomplish liturgically?

Chapter Three

Addressed by the Word

The reading and interpretation of the ancient Scriptures of our faith is a central part of Christian worship. This part of our worship is traced back to the development of the synagogue service during the exile of the Jewish people in Babylon, long before the coming of Christ. To this day, the unrolling of a Torah scroll and its reading or chanting is an essential and dramatic part of Jewish worship. When the early followers of Christ began to develop their own patterns of worship, the presentation of these readings was continued, supplemented by treasured Christian writings, some of which became our New Testament.

Christians are "a people of the book." Our Scriptures are a rich literature, and they provide a history and a heritage. The presentation of Scripture passages and their interpretation in the context of worship is vital for the spiritual nurture and theological education of the entire congregation. For this reason, it is important that we be offered a healthy diet of readings from the Scriptures as a central part of Christian worship. One short reading to provide a text for the sermon is simply not enough to nourish our spirits.

The issue of what passages of Scripture are to be included in a service of worship is easily answered by the use of the Revised Common Lectionary.[1] This is an ecumenically developed listing of Scripture passages for every Sunday and special day of the Christian year over a three-year cycle. In each of the three years, the lectionary moves through one of the Synoptic Gospels—Matthew, Mark, or Luke. The Gospel of John is included each year for special days and seasons. In addition, there are selections from the Old Testament, other parts of the New Testament, and a Psalm to be read or sung for each Lord's Day. There are many advantages to following this plan, one of which is that it *is* a plan. Sundays come in relentless succession, and at the very least, it is good to have a place to start in planning ahead for upcoming Sundays. The lectionary also ensures that, over time, the congregation hears from the full breadth of the Bible. If a congregation or pastor chooses not to follow the lectionary, it is imperative that worship planners and preachers find other means of tending to the full breadth of Scripture. The worship leader, the worship committee, or the program staff should decide on the Scripture passages to be used in the coming weeks or seasons so that music and other worship elements may be planned and coordinated with the theme of the service.

Whatever the number of Scripture passages used, it makes sense to have them read or presented in quick succession immediately after the gathering ritual. This is a way of saying, "This is why we are here. Scripture is central, so let's get right to it." The Scripture passages will likely present themes that can be reiterated and reinforced in other parts of the service, such as hymns, prayers, and responses. Coordinated in this way, spiritual and theological insights may begin to form connections for the congregation, giving new insights, motivation, and encouragement for living as disciples of Jesus Christ.

The sermon should follow as soon as possible after the Scripture readings without a lot of intervening elements of worship in order to make clear and strong the connection between sermon and Scripture. The sermon should be an exposition of a theme from those Scripture passages. It is an invitation, a call, that we need to hear, internalize, and answer with our lives. The sermon is rightly thought of as a conversation between the preacher and the community of faith. It is appropriate following the service for congregants to share with the preacher how the Scripture readings and the sermon and other parts of the service informed and encouraged their own thinking and living as disciples of Jesus Christ. This is a two-way conversation that can continue over the years. The point is not how good or bad we judge the preaching to be, but how our worship together shapes our life and faith.

The Scriptures and the sermon combine to challenge us to embody an ancient faith going back to the early church's witness to the good news announced by Jesus, and beyond that to the story of God's people narrated in the Hebrew Scriptures. There is a huge gap between the cultures reflected in those Scriptures and the cultures of the world in which we live today. It is helpful to acknowledge in some way the immensity of this stretch between Word and world. Otherwise, we may regard our religious heritage as something not just challenging but impossible for us to live up to faithfully. To move from the culture in which we are embedded, which is essentially our secular formation, to a life shaped by the spiritual heritage of the people of God is a significant movement of growth, whether it happens suddenly or over a lifetime.

In this important part of our order of worship, we are not only addressed by the Word but also invited to respond to what we hear. It is not, and cannot be, a one-way street. It is a conversation that forms us as disciples of Jesus the Christ. Yes, we listen, but we also respond in prayers and hymns and responses that place ourselves, our church, and the whole world in the presence of a gracious and loving God. We listen, but we also give of our possessions and our lives in response to the gospel. We listen, but we also confess our faith and commit ourselves to witness and service.

Certainly the service of worship should include prayers of intercession or prayers of the people led by a pastor or member of the congregation. This prayer is also referred to as the pastoral prayer, as it often addresses the pastoral needs and concerns of the people of the congregation. It is a common misunderstanding that this prayer belongs to the pastor. The use of the term *prayers of the people* helps correct this misunderstanding. It is not necessary for the prayer always to be led by a pastor. The prayer should not be a sermon in disguise. It is directed to God and not to the congregation. No matter who leads this prayer, it is always a prayer on behalf of the congregation. That may be made clearer if the prayer includes a vocal response by the congregation such as "Lord, hear our prayer." The "Amen" at the conclusion of the prayer should be spoken by the entire congregation, indicating that we are assenting to the prayer, that we are involved in the prayer, and that we are claiming it as our own prayer.

The offering is best understood as the congregation's

joyful response to the grace of God in Jesus Christ. It is a significant act of worship and should be treated as such. It is an expression of our self-giving in response to God's far more complete self-giving for us and for the world. It is not merely a collection to cover expenses for the church, or some sort of price of admission, or a reluctant duty. Offering of tithes and financial resources is one of the important expressions of our response. The offering also includes the offering of our time, intentions, and spiritual gifts to the ongoing work of God in the world. In addition to placing money, checks, or offering envelopes in baskets or offering plates, the congregation might also place in those baskets or offering plates slips of paper that indicate a giving of self and time for upcoming ministry projects as well as a commitment to pray for the church and the world.

In addition to prayers and the offering, this is an appropriate time in the worship service for an invitation to persons wishing to make a commitment to Christian faith. It is also an appropriate place in the service for a congregational affirmation of faith, for baptism, for confirmation, and for a variety of other acts that express our response to the gospel. Through such acts of worship, the good news of Christ continues to meet us in the living of our lives and invites us into participation with Christ in the life of the world.

Questions for Reflection

1. The Revised Common Lectionary is used by a broad variety of denominations and congregations. What advantages and/or disadvantages do you see in using this resource?

2. Is the centrality of Scripture and the proclamation of its meaning apparent in your service of worship? Are there ways to make the Word more central?
3. In what ways do you ensure that children feel addressed by the Word in ways appropriate and accessible to them?

Chapter Four

The Joyful Feast

Addressed by the Word, responding with gratitude, and claiming our identity in Jesus Christ, we move to the Table. At the Table, we affirm that Christ is present with us as we share the bread broken and the wine poured. This is the "joyful feast of the people of God."[1] Familiar names for this meal are *Communion* and the *Lord's Supper*. Another term is *Eucharist*, a word from the Greek meaning "to give thanks." *Eucharist* expresses something that is often missing and needs to be vigorously restored—a genuine sense of joy that Christ is present and gives himself to us at Table.

In thinking about the Lord's Supper and planning for its celebration, it is helpful to distinguish clearly between the Last Supper and the Lord's Supper. The Last Supper was the meal Jesus shared with his disciples just before he was executed by the Roman government; it anticipated his coming death on the cross. The Lord's Supper celebrates the presence of the risen Christ, victorious over sin and death and present with us now. "Death has been swallowed up in victory" (1 Cor. 15:54). It is significant that after the crucifixion, the risen Christ took bread, gave thanks, broke it, and gave it to his two companions who walked with him on the road to Emmaus. It was then that "their eyes were opened, and they recognized him" (Luke 24:31).

If the Lord's Supper is celebrated as a funeral for Jesus, it should be no surprise that few people are interested in sharing it frequently. Such a service focuses on the sad news of the Last Supper. But as the *Book of Common Worship* of the Presbyterian Church (U.S.A.) explains, a eucharistic celebration of the Lord's Supper recognizes that Jesus not only was crucified for us but also rose for us and is present with us: "While the meaning of Christ's sacrificial death is at the heart of the sacrament, it is a resurrected, living Christ whom we encounter through the bread and the wine."[2] Think about it this way: if Jesus had not been resurrected, there would be no Christian faith. Christians often focus too much on the crucifixion, when Jesus' resurrection is what began the Christian community. We celebrate his resurrection and God's power to overcome powers of death with life when we celebrate Communion.

If this is true, our celebration of Communion should be joyful. Music, prayers, movements, and gestures should fully express the joy of the gospel. We don't celebrate other joyful events such as birthdays, victories, achievements, and anniversaries with passive postures, downcast eyes, folded hands, and dirges sung to mournful tunes. We should evaluate celebrations of the Lord's Supper with this in mind. The use of joyful hymns and triumphant instrumental music is theologically very appropriate. Let's celebrate Christ's risen presence with eucharistic joy. The Lord is risen!

Our celebration of the Lord's Supper needs to be interactive, responsive, and participatory. The Great Prayer of Thanksgiving is itself a corporate prayer, with roots stretching back deep within early Christian tradition, in which the whole congregation participates verbally (and often vocally in song). The prayer is introduced by a traditional responsive dialogue begun by the pastor or celebrant:

> The Lord be with you.
> *And also with you.*
>
> Lift up your hearts.
> *We lift them to the Lord.*
>
> Let us give thanks to the Lord our God.
> *It is right to give our thanks and praise.*

The Great Prayer then begins by giving thanks for creation and for God's mighty acts through the history of God's people. As God's people gathered in worship, we respond by praising God, singing or saying:

> Holy, holy, holy Lord, God of power and might,
> heaven and earth are full of your glory,
> Hosanna in the highest.
> Blessed is he who comes in the name of the Lord.
> Hosanna in the highest.

The presider continues with the prayer, remembering the birth, life, death, and resurrection of Jesus. Then the congregation responds by singing or saying this or another acclamation:

> Christ has died,
> Christ is risen,
> Christ will come again.

The Great Prayer continues by calling on the Holy Spirit to lift us into Christ's presence, to unite us with all the faithful in heaven and earth, to nourish us with the body of Christ, to keep us faithful as Christ's body, and to anticipate the fulfillment of the kingdom proclaimed by Christ. The Great Prayer concludes with the congregation saying or singing "Amen." The congregation then joins voices in praying together the Lord's Prayer.

Just as the Great Prayer invites active participation by the congregation, the way the meal is served can do the same. When the participants come to the servers to receive the bread and wine, they experience moving together as God's people rather than being passive recipients who are served where they are. For those unable to leave their seats, servers come to them individually. There is personal interaction between server and recipient, with one another, and with Christ in the bread and wine. We come as God's family. We come as Christ's disciples. These are the gifts of God for the people of God, and we are glad!

This joyful feast is no longer seen as an occasional service but as a regular and essential part of our worship together, reflecting the earliest practice of the church. Since the 1960s, major Protestant denominations have been moving toward more frequent celebration of Communion—as frequently as each Lord's Day or at least monthly. On days when the Lord's Supper is not celebrated, the sequence of the service remains the same as when the Lord's Supper is celebrated.[3] On these nonsacramental days, a significant prayer of thanksgiving should be included here, followed as on sacramental days by the Lord's Prayer. In this way, the rhythm of the service remains consistent and familiar for the congregation.

Congregations are likely to schedule Communion

more frequently if it is celebrated as a joyful eucharistic feast rather than as a commemoration of the Last Supper. Keeping the preparation details as simple as possible also helps. All that may be needed is the wine or grape juice in a chalice and a basket full of broken bread. If it were meant to be complicated, Jesus would have prescribed a five-course meal complete with the silver service. Keep it simple. Keep it communal. Keep it joyful!

Questions for Reflection

1. As you celebrate Communion in your congregation, is it more like a Last Supper commemoration or a Lord's Supper (eucharistic) celebration? How might you help enhance the celebration of the risen Christ in the meal?

2. Do words like *interactive*, *responsive*, and *participatory* describe Communion as celebrated in your congregation? What would help to make it more so?

3. How does your tradition provide for extending the celebration of Communion to those who are homebound or in the hospital?

Chapter Five

Sent to Serve

Our worship is coming to its culmination. All that remains is a hymn, a charge, and a benediction (literally, a good word). This seems simple enough, but it is filled with significance. We have celebrated Christ, truly present in Word and sacrament. What now? As the disciples Peter, James, and John were called to follow Jesus back down the Mount of Transfiguration into the ordinariness of everyday life to serve as his disciples (Mark 9:2–10), so are we sent back into the world to serve as his disciples.

The final section of worship is more than a mere ending or closing. We are not simply dismissed to participate in the coffee hour or to go out to brunch. We are sent to serve:

> God calls the church to join the mission of Christ in service to the world. As the church engages in that mission, it bears witness to God's reign over all of life. God sends the church in the power of the Holy Spirit to proclaim the gospel, to engage in works of

> compassion and reconciliation, to strive for peace
> and justice in its own life and in the world, to be
> stewards of creation and of life, caring for creation
> until the day when God will make all things new."[1]

This is God's call to the church, not just to the clergy or
to the denominational hierarchy or to a few outstanding
saintly Christians. Our being sent from worship is a regular reminder that we all share this calling, and that our
participation in worship and in the life of the church is to
equip us all for this common ministry (Eph. 4:11–13). It
is important, then, that we heed this reminder and take
it to heart. We have spent this time together not to be
entertained or amused but to be equipped.

We have already mentioned that effective worship
invites the active participation of every worshiper. Now
as the service comes to an end, we are sent to participate in God's kingdom through our relationships and our
actions. The opportunities for each person to embody the
reign of God in the world are as unique as each person's
life situation. There are many situations when each of us
is called to stand alone as a witness, and there are many
other opportunities for us to work together as a congregation or in the larger church to represent the coming of
the kingdom of God in the church and in the world.

Like any other human organization, a congregation
can become inward looking. It is a normal sociological
process that affects all sorts of groups. But against the pull
of this constant gravitational force, the gospel of Christ is
working through the Spirit to turn the church inside out.[2]
The call of Christ is the centrifugal force that sends us
out into the world in mission, in witness, and in service,
beginning near at hand and extending to all the world.

The rhythm of gathering together and then being sent

out in service is the natural rhythm of the Christian life and of the church. This missional calling not only sends some to distant mission fields but also sends us to all the places where we live and work, where we relate to all sorts of people and to all sorts of issues all week long. We are sent back into the world that is the context of our lives, and there we are to model and share the purposes that Jesus taught and lived—and for which he gave up his life. Consider this traditional charge to the congregation:

> Go out into the world in peace;
> have courage;
> hold on to what is good;
> return no one evil for evil;
> strengthen the fainthearted;
> support the weak, and help the suffering;
> honor all people;
> love and serve the Lord,
> rejoicing in the power of the Holy Spirit.[3]

This charge is very pointed: go out in the power of the Spirit to be disciples of Jesus Christ and God's church in the world. The pastor or other worship leader may also frame a charge that is based on the needs and challenges of that particular congregation and of that particular community, or one that comes directly out of the message of the Scripture for the day.

The call to service as Christ's church in the world may also be expressed through recognition of specific avenues of witness and service undertaken by members of the congregation. Such service might be to participate in a particular form of Christian mission or to become a deacon or Stephen Minister or to tutor children in a local school. This not only recognizes those whom the church blesses, prays over, and ordains or commissions but also serves as an example and inspiration to others to do the same.

Questions for Reflection

1. Where does the missional calling to your congregation send you to work and witness for the gospel of Jesus Christ?
2. In what ways might your congregation be described as inward looking rather than outward serving? What might be done to change that?
3. What elements of your worship service express the church's missional calling?

Chapter Six

Music and the Arts in Worship

So far in our worship conversation we have reflected on the basic structure of the Lord's Day service. The basic movements of the service provide a structure and an internal logic that invites us to engage, through the liturgy, in an experience that opens us to God's presence, God's Word in Scripture and sacraments, and God's sending us into the world as disciples of Jesus Christ. When combined with words and liturgical actions, the structure of worship engages us in ways that can be transformative and inspiring.

The service of worship should be a multisensory event. What we hear, what we see, what we taste, and what we touch all combine to offer us moments when mind, body, and spirit are nurtured and fed in deep and powerful ways. This is especially true when music and the arts are well integrated into the worship service. In this chapter, we will reflect on music, movement, visual arts, and technology in the worship service.

Perhaps no other area of modern worship life is as divisive as music. Congregations and worship leaders often battle over whether music in worship should be traditional or contemporary. Pipe organ or piano? Choir or praise team? Brass quartet or jazz combo? In *Beyond the Worship Wars*, Thomas Long explores contemporary tensions in congregational worship in an effort to move us beyond the bickering and battling that inhibits engaging and dynamic worship. In the course of the book, Long names several characteristics of vital and faithful congregations, one of which is particularly relevant for us: "Vital and faithful congregations emphasize congregational music that is both excellent and eclectic in style and genre."[1]

Music in worship is not an end unto itself. Music in worship is meant to invite the congregation to participate in ways that inspire and nurture. This happens when we listen to preludes played on an organ, anthems sung by a choir, offertories rung by handbells, or musical works played by instrumentalists of all varieties and configurations who offer their praise and worship on our behalf. Musicians (professional, avocational, amateur, and recreational) offer their gifts in ways that inspire and nurture a listening congregation.

Beyond simply providing listening opportunities for a congregation, instrumental music and vocal music have the ability to move us through the liturgy in ways (often subconscious) that unite the liturgical elements of the worship service and foster an experience that can speak deeply to our hearts and souls.

The primary role of instrumentalists and vocalists in worship, though, is to facilitate the participation of the congregation in offering its own songs to God. From our beginnings in ancient Israel, to the early church, and throughout Christian history, congregational singing has included hymns, psalms, and spiritual songs. Hymns are metrical compositions adapted for singing praise to God. Songs include a variety of nonmetrical compositions. In our services of worship, congregations often sing several hymns or songs along with various pieces of service music (a Kyrie, a doxology, or an amen, for example). At no time in the history of the church have we had available to us such a variety of congregational song.

To be honest, though, the variety can be a bit over-whelming. Look in the index of any mainline denomina-tion's hymnal or songbook published in the last twenty years and you will find early church chants, Reformation-era chorales and hymns, early American folk tunes, nineteenth-century gospel hymns, African American spirituals, contemporary Christian praise and worship choruses, short songs from the Taizé and Iona commu-nities, and hymns and songs from around the world in languages, rhythms, and styles very different from one another. The variety, while initially overwhelming, is also an exciting gift to the church. Congregational sing-ing has the ability to unite our hearts and voices not only with those with whom we sing in worship but also with the church through all times and in all places.

The variety of congregational song speaks to Long's observation that vital and faithful congregations experi-ence music that is eclectic in style and genre. Rather than settling for overly simplistic divisions into traditional and contemporary—remembering that those terms are as relative as the hearer's own experiences—congregations should strive for singing experiences that blend a variety of styles and genres together (chorale tunes, spirituals, global music, praise and worship choruses, etc.). For those planning and leading worship, careful attention should be paid to how music is used in the service of the liturgy, what the genre and style requirements are for a particular piece, and how a congregation is invited, instructed, and supported in its fullest participation.

Long also mentions excellence of music for vital and faithful congregations. Nothing frustrates a congregation's musical experience in worship more than music played or sung poorly. Musicians and music leaders of whatever ability should devote adequate preparation and practice for worship not only in their directing, the playing of their instrument, or their singing but also in the intentionality with which they will involve the congregation in singing.

For a congregation that is expanding its repertoire of congregational song into new and varying styles and genres, the introduction and support of singing is critical. It is helpful to take a long-term view of increasing this repertoire. Rather than overwhelm a congregation with new hymns and songs each week, consider limiting how much new music is included in any particular service. If you typically sing three hymns or songs, for example, make sure that two of the three are familiar to the congregation. It is best for the congregation to begin and end the service with familiar hymns and songs.

New songs need intentional and thoughtful introduction. This might include playing them instrumentally or having them sung by the choir or a soloist a week or two in advance of the congregation's singing them for the first time. Perhaps the choir or soloist could sing the first verse of a new hymn and invite the congregation to join on the remaining verses. If the song is in a verse-refrain format, the choir or soloist might sing all the verses, with the congregation singing only the refrain. Short songs that are meant to be repeated (Taizé songs, praise and worship choruses, some global songs) need to be given time to settle into the voice of the congregation. It really is OK, and stylistically appropriate, to repeat something more than once! Whatever their instrument, accompanists need to be sure the melody is prominent and that their accompaniments support rather than frustrate the congregation. This is all part of excellence, as much as playing the right notes and rhythms.

Because of recent technological advances, the presentation of songs to a congregation no longer assumes the use of a hymnal or songbook with notes and music. That said, hymnals and songbooks do offer the worshiper the ability to see a melody's trajectory (whether the notes move up or down, how the words correspond to the rhythm, etc.). Whenever possible, a visual resource of words *and* music is helpful to a congregation. If hymnals or songbooks are not available, perhaps inserts or handouts can be provided (following applicable copyright provisions, of course.)

Some congregations have made the decision to project words on a screen for congregational singing. When hymns and songs are familiar to a congregation or simple in construction so that people can pick them up quickly by ear, screens often facilitate good singing experiences, especially because people's heads are not buried in a book. But using a screen or using a hymnal or songbook need not be an either/or decision. Screens and hymnals or songbooks can both be employed at the same time, giving worshipers an option of which medium will best facilitate their singing. Offering hymnals, songbooks, or inserts while using a screen as the primary technology for congregational singing also provides ensurance that the congregation will still be able to sing even when computers freeze, projector bulbs burn out, or someone forgets to load the PowerPoint presentation.

Music is an integral part of the worship service—congregational singing especially so. Music as an art engages the heart, mind, and soul in ways that often mediate an experience of the holy. As worship seeks to inspire a deepened faith that equips us to be ever more faithful disciples of Jesus Christ, music serves worship well.

Music is not the only art form that has the ability to enhance our worship experience. Closely related to music is the natural expression of movement with music. Liturgical dance can be a meaningful addition to worship. Certain scriptural texts, hymns, and songs lend themselves particularly well to dance. Thoughtful and appropriate choreography, adequate rehearsal, and care to be sure dance and dancers draw attention to worship rather than to themselves can lead to meaningful experiences of liturgical dance. Excellence in dance is as essential as excellence in music.

Visual arts can also enhance the congregation's worship experience. Certain colors are used in worship throughout the year to communicate the rhythm of the liturgical calendar. Those colors (purple/blue, white, green, and red) find common expression in the use of various paraments in a worship space. Paraments include a variety of liturgical hangings and cloths used around altars, Communion tables, pulpits, and lecterns. Complementing paraments are stoles worn by clergy and worship leaders. The colors and the symbols used in paraments and stoles engage the visual senses of the worshiper and enrich the worship experience. (For more on the use of colors in worship, see chap. 13.)

Many congregations also find the introduction and use

of banners a helpful visual enhancement of worship. Banners come in all shapes and sizes. They can be purchased from a variety of sources, or they can be created and produced by a congregation. As with paraments, symbols and words used on banners can engage people with more of their senses and contribute to their reflection on the life of Christian faith. Banners designed and created from within a congregation also allow gifts and skills to be used in a way that directly contributes to the congregation's worship life. Someone who may not be comfortable singing in a choir or reading Scripture might very well enjoy sewing symbols onto a banner that will be used in worship.

While paraments, stoles, and banners enhance worship in subtle and unspoken ways, they also offer one of the more natural entry points into worship education. Take Pentecost, for example. This particular Sunday invites congregations to read, remember, and celebrate the gift of the Holy Spirit to the gathered disciples as recorded in the book of Acts. The liturgical color for Pentecost is red. Imagine walking into a worship space and seeing red in paraments and stoles worn by the choir. Perhaps the paraments include the image of a descending dove. A banner hung behind the lectern includes a depiction of the disciples with tongues of flame over their heads and the citation Acts 2:1–3. The visual sense is engaged. Perhaps the banner will cause worshipers to open their Bibles and read the text:

> When the day of Pentecost had come, they were all together in one place. And suddenly from heaven there came a sound like the rush of a violent wind, and it filled the entire house where they were sitting.

Divided tongues, as of fire, appeared among them,
and a tongue rested on each of them. (Acts 2:1–3)

In the bulletin or within the service itself (such as in
the sermon or children's sermon), the liturgical color can
be explained as well as the identity of the descending dove
and the tongues of fire as images of the Holy Spirit. The
thoughtful use of visual arts can leave deep and lasting
impressions for a worshiper.

The visual arts, dance, and music are elements of worship that have the ability to engage the hearts, minds,
and spirits of those who worship. Week in and week out,
music and the arts can bring creativity, energy, and fresh-
ness to the dependable liturgical structure that is always
shaping and forming us as God's people.

Questions for Reflection

1. Can you name an experience when a hymn, song,
   or instrumental piece in worship moved you?
2. As you look in the index of your congregation's
   hymnal or songbook, what variety of hymns and
   songs do you see?
3. Close your eyes and visualize your worship space.
   What paraments, stoles, and banners do you see?
   Do you know what they symbolize or communicate?
4. Who in your congregation has gifts related to
   visual arts? Music? Dance? Are they contributing
   their gifts and skills to your congregation's worship
   experience? If not, how can you encourage them
   to do so?

Chapter Seven

Worship for Special Times

Gathering for worship each Lord's Day is the church's most ancient practice. Throughout history, this weekly pattern has typically followed the same general order: gathering, Word, joyful feast, and sending. This day and this worship order are basic to our formation as a community of God's people.

Alongside this pattern of worship each Lord's Day, there also developed from earliest times another pattern: an annual calendar of special days and seasons to celebrate central aspects of Christ's redemptive work. Two of these special days and seasons developed very early in the history of the church. Christmas celebrates God's incarnation in Christ. Easter celebrates our redemption through Christ's death and resurrection. In later centuries, other days and seasons were added, some of which served either to help worshipers prepare for or reflect on the meaning of Christmas and Easter. Other special days celebrate significant events in the life and ministry of Jesus. They all point us to the centrality of Christ for the worship and life of the church.

As a result of the Puritan political reaction in the early Protestant period, this annual liturgical calendar was suppressed and then largely ignored in England, Scotland, and the American colonies. There was a time when even Christmas and Easter were not observed as special days in Puritan New England. The slow and steady recovery of the liturgical calendar during the twentieth century was a great gift to all denominations from the ecumenical movement. The reform of the liturgical calendar during the Second Vatican Council of the Roman Catholic Church in the 1960s added momentum to developments that had been taking place over many years in several Protestant denominations. The liturgical calendar, now shared across many parts of the whole church, provides a strong theological spine for our worship throughout the year. It unites us in the celebration of special days and seasons "that confront us with who we are in Christ and present us with patterns for growth in Christ."[1]

In recent years, there has been remarkable consensus on the ecumenical liturgical calendar among major Protestant denominations and the Roman Catholic Church. Using the liturgical calendar allows the order of worship to be focused through a kaleidoscope of changing texts, liturgies, and music that is now readily available in print and online for every Sunday of the year. All this is naturally connected to the three-year schedule of weekly readings provided by the Revised Common Lectionary.

Those who are involved in planning a congregation's worship for special days and seasons will be heartened to know that so many resources are available for their work. Collaboration with others can also add creativity and energy to worship planning. For example, solo pastors may find help in sermon planning by meeting regularly with a group of local pastors to study the lectionary together and share ideas for preaching and worship. If distance is an issue, these meetings might also occur by conference call or through online means such as Skype conversations. In other situations, pastors can encourage program staff to bring various resources to worship planning meetings or retreats. In some congregations, resources might be shared with the worship committee, musicians, and others as they join the pastor in worship planning.

Serious and imaginative worship planning for special days and seasons helps to keep a congregation focused on the central aspects of the gospel message and on what it means to belong to Christ. A well-executed plan for these special times enables those who do the worship planning to present the gospel message in ways that are both effective and spiritually nurturing for those who worship.

Initially, the liturgical calendar may seem a daunting list of days and seasons with names such as Advent, Epiphany, Lent, and Pentecost—names more familiar to theologically trained leaders than to most church members. Actually, the liturgical calendar isn't really all that complicated; most of the special seasons and days of worship are a part of either the Christmas cycle or the Easter cycle.

In the next few chapters, we will explore the seasons of Christmas and Easter. Each is a cluster or cycle of celebrations that includes an extended time of preparation followed by a special day that ushers in a new season. In the case of both of these seasons (Christmas and Easter), we suggest considering first the history and meaning of the primary season (Christmas and Easter), and then the associated seasons of preparation (Advent and Lent). In this way the seasons of preparation may more effectively and appropriately fit the meaning and purpose of the primary season. In other words, think of Christmas Eve or Easter morning as the destination toward which you want your congregation to be moving, and then plan Advent or Lent to be the kind of preparation that people will need to reach those destinations in meaningful ways. Other special liturgical days will be explored after the exploration of the Christmas and Easter cycles.

Questions for Reflection

1. Can you imagine church without Christmas or Easter or Pentecost? What does the calendar of feasts and festivals add to the life of the church?
2. In what ways does the liturgical calendar of special days and seasons "present us with patterns of growth in Christ"?
3. Who in your congregation is involved in planning for seasons like Advent and Lent? What is the process for planning these times?

Chapter Eight

Celebrating Christmas
(and Epiphany)

What exactly is Christmas? What is its essential message? Before we can know how to celebrate Advent (the season of preparation for Christmas), we must form a clearer perception of what Christmas means for the life of the church. In our culture, multiple Christmases coexist side by side. There is the commercial Christmas, the cultural Christmas, the ethnic Christmas, the family Christmas, the office-party Christmas, the church Christmas, and more. The Christmas that we celebrate may be a complex blend of them all.

Christmas is generally understood to be the celebration of the birth of Jesus. But the actual date of Jesus' birth is not known and probably not knowable. It is likely that December 25 was originally chosen to coincide with the Roman holiday Saturnalia, marking the Northern Hemisphere's winter solstice, when the dark days of winter began to give way to longer, brighter days, promising spring. By 336 CE, churches in Rome were observing December 25 as Christmas, the day to celebrate the coming of Christ to be the "light of the world."

For the church, Christmas celebrates Emmanuel, "God with us," fulfilled in the birth, ministry, death, and resurrection of Jesus the Christ. Christmas celebrates the affirmation that "in Christ God was reconciling the world to himself" (2 Cor. 5:19). British theoretical physicist and theologian John Polkinghorne observes, "Christmas is the time when we mark and celebrate the beginning of the great revelatory act of the *incarnation*" (emphasis added).[1] He also comments, "The doctrine of the incarnation . . . did not arise out of ungrounded speculation but out of the undeniable character of the *encounter* of the first disciples with the post-Easter Christ" (emphasis added).[2]

It is not enough for a congregation simply to settle for a churchly version of the secular Christmas. Christmas is the incarnation of God in human form that we celebrate! A casual mix of Christmas joy and a few old Christmas carols will not do for the church's celebration of this wonderful and significant festival. A predictable and culturally conditioned Christmas is not likely to make a difference in anyone's life. But the incarnation of God, reflected through our own encounter with the living Christ and articulated in our own authentic faith, can make a real difference in someone's life. This is why it is very important to plan the congregation's celebration of Christmas with care and thoroughness.

Though the secular holiday glitters with spectacular displays everywhere we turn, and though the holiday season may awaken a powerful mix of human emotions and relationships, it can wear very thin as we experience too much to do and too little time to do it. Over against all that busyness and glitter, the Christmas we celebrate as the church may offer the beauty of thoughtful theological focus. Let the church's Christmas decor highlight with simplicity the message of God-with-us and the coming of God's light to the whole human family. Candlelight and a rough manger for the Christ child may say incarnation more eloquently than overly elaborate Christmas decorations that mimic the extravagance of the local mall. Let us plan Christmas worship that is theologically grounded and clearly focused on the ultimate meaning of the coming of God in Christ for us all.

What the church does to celebrate this special time should address the spiritual hunger of human beings and of human society. What a shame if a congregation exhausts all its energies producing a Christmas extravaganza while overlooking its own hurts and hungers as well as those of the people who come to church looking for something that connects them to God.

Out of sensitivity for those who are grieving the loss of loved ones during the Christmas season, some congregations offer what is called a Blue Christmas service. In such a service, those who are grieving participate in a simple liturgy of lighting a candle and saying the name of their loved one. Joining in prayers and hymns, they are comforted by the knowledge that they are not alone in their loss. Services of wholeness and healing provide space and opportunity not only for those who grieve but also for those who feel lonely or estranged from family or friends at Christmas. Such services illustrate Christmas planning and programming that responds compassionately to real human and spiritual needs, and they can bring Christmas good news to those who struggle with a variety of issues of wholeness and healing, which so often go unattended amid the Christmas cheer.

Christmas celebrates the nativity of Jesus and has its own unique excitement. Christmas Day is December 25, but its celebration begins the previous evening, Christmas Eve. Christmas continues for twelve days until Epiphany. Christmas Eve should be celebrated splendidly, with carols and choirs and candlelight. It is liturgically fitting to celebrate Communion in at least one of the Christmas Eve services. As Jesus came to us through the physical pain of childbirth, lived a flesh-and-blood human life in this world, and died a physical death on a wooden cross, he is also present with us in the physical gifts of bread and wine. In the words of a fourteenth-century eucharistic hymn, *Ave verum Corpus, natum de Maria Virgine* ("Hail true Body, born of the Virgin Mary"). There may be no better way to celebrate incarnation than to participate in Christmas Eucharist.

Though many congregations limit Christmas services to Christmas Eve, Christmas worship may also be offered on Christmas Day. There are those who simply are not able to worship at any time on Christmas Eve, and they should not be left out. A Christmas morning service might be offered at 11:00 a.m., which is between the typical time when gifts are exchanged and when people may be traveling for a family gathering. Such a service may not be well attended the first year or two, but it will likely grow and be well worth the effort.

The Christmas season ends on Epiphany, which is January 6. Epiphany deserves its own worship celebration. Epiphany comes to us out of the early liturgical practice of the churches of the East. As Christmas celebrates the *sending* of Christ *into* the world, so Epiphany celebrates the *revealing* of Christ *to* the world. Christmas focuses on the birth in the stable. Epiphany focuses on the revealing of Christ to the magi (astrologers from afar), who traveled from a distant place to worship the Christ child. The addition of Epiphany to Christmas strongly suggests that Christmas has a missional consequence for the church. Indeed, any reading of the Acts of the Apostles makes it abundantly clear that the church was and is instrumentally involved in the revealing of Christ to the world through the telling of the gospel story and by living its message. The church as we see it in Acts is not a religious social club. It is a city set on a hill to reveal the light of Christ to the world. As the church, we are called to shine the light of Christ into all places. Our Christmas and Epiphany celebrations can be profound and exciting ways to do just that.

Questions for Reflection

1. How does Christmas as currently celebrated in your congregation differ from more secular observances of Christmas? How might it contribute to faith formation and maturing Christian discipleship?
2. How might what you plan for Christmas make a pastorally sensitive difference in the lives of those in your congregation and community who are experiencing difficult times?
3. What might your congregation do to celebrate or enhance your current celebration of Epiphany?

Chapter Nine

Advent as Preparation

We turn now to consider the season that precedes Christmas and Epiphany. Advent is a season of preparation. It is a season of expectant hope. Though the lectionary readings for one of the Sundays of Advent speak of judgment and of end-times, such passages serve to point us to the ultimate fulfillment of God's loving purpose working itself out even beyond history. This is expressed in the promise of Scripture that Jesus will return to the world in some sort of second coming, or second advent. Advent reminds us of God's coming to us not only in the birth, life, and death of Jesus but also in the promise of the *parousia*, of Christ's coming again. In this hope, Advent helps us to make room for Christ in the world and in our own lives here and now.

It is appropriate to begin the Advent season by singing some of the many lovely Advent hymns and songs and to save Christmas carols until closer to Christmas Day. Of course, to promote the commercial Christmas, carols will already have been heard everywhere for quite some time, and some congregants will be anxious to hear them in church right away. But this may be one way that Advent helps the church remain countercultural and distinguish its own Christmas message from all the others. It might be appropriate to sing a Christmas carol or two near the end of Advent, but then sing Christmas carols until Epiphany! This is one way in which Advent has time to prepare us to celebrate and internalize Christmas.

Another way to prepare for the celebration of Christmas and to internalize its profound significance is to add Christmas decorations throughout the church gradually over the season of Advent rather than to have all decorations in place immediately after Thanksgiving. A unique addition to worship during Advent that highlights the season as distinct from Christmas and as a time of fruitful waiting is the incorporation of the Advent wreath in the gathering segment of the congregation's worship. An Advent wreath is a ring of evergreen with four purple or blue candles as part of the ring and a white candle in the center. Each week in the four weeks of Advent a candle is lit. A prominent Advent wreath in worship enables worshipers to count down the weeks of waiting and preparation and to experience the growing presence of the light of Christ coming into the world. Simple liturgy and additional sung responses add to the experience of the Advent wreath for a congregation. On Christmas Eve, the white candle, often called the Christ candle, is also lit to announce the birth of Jesus Christ.

As a season of preparation and expectant hope, Advent is an ideal time to further nurture a congregation spiritually through a variety of means. Advent devotional guides with daily Scripture readings, reflections, and prayers are available from a variety of sources. Many congregations publish their own based on members' own reflections. Covenant groups, small groups of people who gather for prayer and reflection, are a natural fit with Advent. Perhaps an Advent retreat could be offered to allow for focused reflection on the themes of Advent, Christmas, and Epiphany.

Amid the rush of the secular holiday season, Advent gives us a chance to catch our breath. Advent also gives us time to sort out our priorities, to engage in spiritually focused worship, and to participate in personal devotional practices that can help make room for Christ in our lives and in our schedules. In order for Advent to be this kind of season of preparation for Christmas, a congregation's worship committee, pastor, or worship team will need to engage in thoughtful reflection and planning well in advance of Advent's arrival. Consideration needs to be given to the meaning and purpose of the season and not just to what the congregation has done in the past. Local traditions and habits should be examined carefully—and then kept, transformed, or dropped depending on how well they help to form us spiritually as people of God and disciples of Jesus Christ.

Questions for Reflection

1. What can be done to help members of your congregation celebrate Advent as a time for their own personal preparation for God's coming to us in Christ?
2. Who in your congregation does the planning for Advent and Christmas? When is it typically done? How are the musicians and others involved in worship leadership included in the planning?
3. How does your congregation plan the decor of the worship space (and building) for Advent and

Christmas? Who does the decorating for these seasons, and when? How do you distinguish between Advent and Christmas by the way the worship space is decorated?

Chapter Ten

Celebrating Easter

To understand the significance of Lent and Holy Week and to plan for their observance, it is very helpful to begin with a clear understanding of Easter. In approaching Lent and Holy Week in this way, a congregation is more likely to plan these times with Easter clearly in mind. If Easter is a time to enter more fully into the new life promised in the risen Christ, then the purpose of Lent and Holy Week should be to prepare for that experience. For the purpose of understanding and planning Lent and Holy Week, our sequence begins with understanding Easter.

Easter in most Protestant churches is essentially a commemoration of the resurrection of Jesus. It is a very special day, a day of joy and gladness. Members of the congregation will have been busy getting the place of worship clean and beautiful for this special day. Easter flowers in abundance will decorate the sanctuary. There might be an Easter egg hunt for the small children who arrive in their new Easter clothes and carrying their

Easter baskets, and the young people of the church may be hosting an Easter breakfast for the congregation.

"Christ is risen," the worship leader proclaims, and the congregation responds "Christ is risen, indeed!" Special Easter music, rehearsed for weeks, is sung by the choir, perhaps with brass accompaniment. The hope of resurrection to eternal life is proclaimed in a sermon. Joyful Easter hymns are sung by the congregation. It is a glorious morning, although it is too soon replaced by the more mundane rhythms of other spring routines and events.

The death and resurrection of our Lord Jesus Christ is the central mystery at the heart of Christian faith. The church's first celebration of what we have come to call Easter was a Christian adaptation of the ancient Hebrew Passover, which told the story of Israel's liberation from bondage and its call to be God's people. The apostle Paul wrote, "For our paschal lamb, Christ, has been sacrificed. Therefore, let us celebrate the festival" (1 Cor. 5:7b-8a). The ancient church included baptism as initiation into Christ as a part of the ancient Passover festival; in doing so, it affirmed a vital theological connection linking Jesus' death and resurrection to our own new life in Christ. This was celebrated at the Vigil, which was observed on the eve of Easter day.

For the ancient church, Easter (or Pascha) was a significant spiritual event—theologically, personally, and communally. The Paschal Vigil was a life-changing personal transformation for those who had been mentored in a life of faith in Christ over a period of months, sometimes years, and who on the eve of Easter were finally plunged into the "death" of the baptismal pool and raised to a new life in Christ as a part of his church.

This ancient connection linking Easter to baptism has

been lost in most of our congregations, blunting much of Easter's meaning and theological impact. Orthodox professor and liturgical theologian Alexander Schmemann commented as long ago as 1974, "Not many Christians . . . know that the liturgy of Easter is primarily a baptismal liturgy. . . . Not many Christians have been taught that Easter . . . developed originally from baptism."[1] It is time to acknowledge baptism's connection to Easter and to make changes in the way we celebrate Easter. Much is at stake.

Baptism, shaped by the meaning of Christ's death and resurrection, is most clearly expressed in the baptism of adults. The apostle Paul wrote to the church in Rome, "Therefore we have been buried with him by baptism into death, so that, just as Christ was raised from the dead by the glory of the Father, so we too might walk in newness of life" (Rom. 6:4). This language of death and resurrection clearly reflects not the baptism of infants but the baptism of adults by immersion.

The baptismal theology we have inherited from the Reformation assumed for the most part the old baptismal theology of the medieval church. Because that baptismal theology was influenced strongly by Augustine's doctrine of original sin, baptism became a sacrament almost exclusively for the eternal salvation of infants. Within the context of an established Christendom, adults were assumed to already have been baptized and to already be members of the church, leaving only infants, a few local stragglers, and the unevangelized in far-off lands needing to be baptized. That understanding worked well enough as long as society was at least nominally Christian, but that clearly is not our situation today.

This is not to say that the baptism of infants is

theologically less significant. The sacrament of baptism for infants is both meaningful and appropriate when it can reasonably be expected that they will be taught the good news of Jesus Christ at home and will be supported in their faith development and Christian discipleship by a loving and faithful congregation. However, the situation we increasingly confront today is that many adults have had little or no personal experience of a life of faith as part of a congregation. This includes many young adults whom we have baptized in our own congregations but whose baptism was not followed by effective formation in faith either at home or in a congregation.

How do we move from our conventional Easter to an Easter that once again connects with an adult baptismal identity? The advantages of doing so are significant: a more theologically meaningful celebration of Easter, an understanding of baptism appropriate to the actual situation of the church in today's world, and a ministry practice focused on adult inquirers. The transition may not be an easy one, but it will be a significant one for any congregation that is serious about a ministry of outreach to adults, including young adults. Help for developing such a ministry is available as a result of significant liturgical renewal that has taken place internationally and ecumenically. Through the North American Association for the Catechumenate, denominations as varied as Episcopalian, Lutheran, Presbyterian, and Mennonite are working together to shape ministries with adult seekers involving an extended time of faith formation and a meaningful experience of adult baptism at Easter.[2]

The transition to a more theologically vibrant Easter can best be done over a number of years. As a first step, a congregation could plan a new member class to take place during Lent, with the reception of new members to take place on Easter Sunday morning. If there is the possibility of one or more adult baptisms among those new members, those baptisms may take place at the Easter service. This can be an opportunity for the congregation to begin to connect Easter with baptism and adult discipleship. If there are no candidates for baptism on Easter Sunday, one step that can still be taken is to include a reaffirmation of baptism as part of the Easter service.

In the second year, a congregation might reshape the new member class to be more about discipleship and less about membership. Giving it a new name can help: something like the Faith and Life class or the Journey of Faith group or Discipleship Formation. As you begin to plan for this new venture, make a special effort to recruit young adults and to shape the curriculum or class discussions to respond to their needs and questions. Schedule the process to begin well before Lent but to finish again at Easter. Enrich the program with new elements. Consider asking faithful and mature members of your congregation to serve as sponsors or companions for each prospective member. If there has been a confirmation class, consider scheduling those confirmations and/or baptisms to take place at the Easter Sunday service.

In the third year, you might consider an Easter Vigil service. This is a service on the Saturday evening before Easter. The service begins outside the church building with the congregation gathered around a new fire representing Christ's resurrection. It continues with a procession into the church building as part of the service of light. This is followed by the service of the Word, the service of Baptism, and the service of the Lord's Supper. The Vigil is a rich and glorious pilgrimage of sorts that moves from place to place in and out of the church building. The service of the Word tells the story of our calling to belong to God's people through biblical passages read or enacted in a variety of imaginative ways. It evokes the religious imagination of both young and old, and it makes clear the connection of Easter to baptism and to the Lord's Supper. Most Protestant denominations now have contemporary versions of this ancient Easter Vigil service.

Whether or not a congregation ultimately decides to offer an Easter Vigil, what is most important is to celebrate Easter in ways that link Easter to adult baptism. That can be started by including adult baptism as often as possible at every Easter service and by highlighting the faith journey of the adults who come to be baptized.

An important difference between the Easter celebrated by the ancient church and our Easter without baptism is that ours feels more remote from our actual lives—a scene we observe from a distance. Our contemporary Easter focuses more on what happened back then and back there and not so much on our own journeys into a faith relationship here and now. Contrast this with the following affirmation by liturgical scholar Aidan Kavanagh: "Baptism is not an enacted metaphor based on the cross: baptism is the power of the cross made actual among those who believe."[3]

As those belonging to mainline Protestant congregations, we often feel that we do not know how to evangelize. At the same time, we lament our congregation's lack of growth and vitality and its failure to attract young adults to a life of faith as a part of the church. What a difference it makes in the life of a congregation when Easter becomes not just a commemoration of Jesus' resurrection but also the celebration of a growing edge of faith among the members of that congregation.

Questions for Reflection

1. What does it mean to commemorate something? What do you believe is the difference between commemorating Easter and experiencing Easter as a life-changing transformation?

2. Have you thought of Easter as primarily a baptismal celebration? What would it mean to think of baptism as a symbol of your own death and resurrection spiritually?

3. What steps would be necessary for your congregation to move toward an Easter celebration that once again connected Easter to baptism and to an adult awareness of baptismal identity in Christ?

Chapter Eleven

Lent and Holy Week: Journeying with Christ

Lent is a period of preparation for Easter lasting forty days (excluding Sundays). Lent begins with the service for Ash Wednesday. It is critical to make this solemn service a significant beginning for Lent that calls each of us to begin a Lenten discipline in preparation for the good news of Easter. When the imposition of ashes is included in this service, we hear God's statement in Genesis 3:19: "You are dust, and to dust you shall return." This is a blunt reminder of our mortality. It is also an urgent invitation to contemplate the death of our old self-centered life and the beginning of our new life in Christ in the assurance that "we belong in life and in death to our faithful savior, Jesus Christ."[1]

Lent is a kind of pilgrimage or journey. Such a journey calls for simplifying things and for traveling light. It is a time for each of us to ask, "What helps me live my faith, and what just gets in the way?" Lent is a good time to begin or to enrich devotional reading and prayer disciplines. Lent is a good time to serve the poor and to work for justice. Lent is a good time for a spiritual retreat that includes silence, prayer, reflection, and worship. Lent is a good time to ask, "Is my identity rooted in faith, baptism, and discipleship, or is it rooted in something else? If it's rooted in something else, what do I need to do about that?" Lent is a time to live into a new way of being, with God's help.

Lenten worship opportunities such as morning, midday, or evening prayer services can nurture our journey or pilgrimage through this season. Simply providing times for personal reflection in the worship space(s) of your congregation without planned liturgy is also an important element of Lent. Additionally, daily devotional materials; covenant groups; special studies to read and reflect on the meaning of Christ's life, death, and resurrection; and congregational retreats can make the Lenten journey a rich one indeed.

The focus of Holy Week is the death of Jesus Christ. It begins with Palm Sunday, which is also referred to as Palm/Passion Sunday. In addition to the triumphal entry at the beginning of worship, the passion of Christ may become the focus of this service as it nears its end. This is especially helpful for churches that find it difficult to offer other services during Holy Week. This combined Palm/Passion emphasis avoids the possibility of a story line that skips directly from triumphal entry to resurrection and so bypasses the cross.

Lent and Holy Week come to an intense conclusion the three days before Easter Sunday (referred to in some traditions as the *Triduum*). Maundy Thursday celebrates the gift of the Lord's Supper and the call of Christ for us to live lives of humble service to others. The word *Maundy* comes from the Latin *mandatum*—"mandate" or "commandment"—referring to Jesus' words, "I give you a new commandment, that you love one another. Just as I have loved you, you also should love one another" (John 13:34). Maundy Thursday includes the observance of the sacrament of the Lord's Supper. It is not to be celebrated as a *Last* Supper, because this evening we can rejoice in the gift of this holy meal in which Jesus promised to be with us. We can also hear and heed his call to love and serve others, the least and the lost, by reading and/or enacting the story of Jesus' washing the feet of his disciples.

Good Friday (which is derived from the Middle English "God's Friday") marks Jesus' death on the cross. Traditionally, the passion narrative is read in its entirety, often from the Gospel of John (18:1–19:42). The worship space is generally stripped bare of flowers, paraments, and other decorations. A rough cross may be placed in the worship space, perhaps draped in a black cloth. Communion is *not* celebrated on Good Friday. The service ends with no benediction, no good bidding. With the death of Jesus remembered, the liturgy simply ends. The decrease of light in the worship space can also enhance the mood and focus of the service.

The evening of Holy Saturday is the time for the Paschal Vigil (see chap. 10), and it is regarded as the first service of Easter. Maundy Thursday, Good Friday, and Holy Saturday are distinct in their focus. Together they form the heart of Holy Week and lead us into a deeper celebration of Easter. As a journey or pilgrimage, they should not be combined into one service on either Thursday or Friday; rather, they stand on their own as significant moments in the journey.

From all that we have said about Lent, Holy Week, and Easter, it is obvious that a meaningful and effective celebration of these special times requires attention and

advance planning by the pastor(s), staff, worship committee, and others who will be involved in positions of
worship leadership. Careful and creative planning, begun
early enough and involving all the participants, will help
to make all these celebrations meaningful and inspiring.
Given the importance of these days and seasons, it is also
helpful to evaluate the experiences soon after Easter, with
notes and observations kept for future reference in the
planning of the next year's journey through Lent, Holy
Week, and Easter.

Questions for Reflection

1. If Lent is a sort of pilgrimage or journey to Easter,
   what resources would you want to provide to your
   congregation for the journey? What Lenten activities might help members prepare themselves for a
   rich and transformative Easter?
2. What services are typical for your congregation
   for Ash Wednesday and the special days of Holy
   Week? How might your typical services be rein-
   vigorated and their importance stressed for faith
   formation and Christian discipleship?
3. How does your congregation plan the decor of
   your worship space for Lent, Holy Week, and Easter? Who does the decorating, and when? How
   might you distinguish clearly between Lent, Holy
   Week, and Easter by the way the worship space is
   decorated?

Chapter Twelve

The Great Fifty Days
of Easter and Pentecost
Day—Celebration Overflowing

Easter ends too soon in most Protestant congregations. The day of resurrection is soon over, and Easter is relegated to no more than a single day. There needs
to be more time for the astonishing message "Christ is
risen" to sink into our lives and form us as Easter people.

Contrary to popular belief or practice, there *is* more
time in the liturgical year to celebrate and internalize
Easter. There is a whole season of seven weeks (fifty days)
linking Easter to the day of Pentecost, and it is by no
means ordinary time. On the contrary, it is the summit
of the liturgical year, calling us from the cross and the
empty tomb to the outpouring of the Holy Spirit and the
birth of the church. This season is an opportune time to
encourage your congregants to reflect on the meaning of
Easter and their own baptismal identity and to discover
how the meaning of Easter and baptism might mature
and deepen the Spirit-led discipleship of their own lives.

So let's not have Easter die on Easter Sunday! Continue to celebrate Jesus' resurrection. Continue to sing
Easter songs and hymns with allusions to the promise

of new life. Interpret Easter not just as an event of history to commemorate but as a continuing spiritual reality with the power to transform. Think of Easter not only as something to celebrate but also as something to practice. Make these weeks a special time. Consider offering the Lord's Supper on each of the seven Sundays of Easter. Offer a weekend retreat. Let the message of Easter joined to Pentecost stimulate your religious imagination and that of the congregation.

The final Sunday of the Easter season is Pentecost. This day has its roots in the worship of ancient Israel. The word *Pentecost* comes from their observance of Shavuot, the Feast of Weeks, which was celebrated fifty days after Passover. It literally means the fiftieth day. It was on the day of this ancient festival that the Holy Spirit came down on the followers of Jesus in Jerusalem.

> When the day of Pentecost had come, they were all together in one place. And suddenly from heaven there came a sound like the rush of a violent wind, and it filled the entire house where they were sitting. Divided tongues, as of fire, appeared among them, and a tongue rested on each of them. All of them were filled with the Holy Spirit and began to speak in other languages, as the Spirit gave them ability. (Acts 2:1-4)

> Peter said to them, "Repent, and be baptized every one of you in the name of Jesus Christ so that your sins may be forgiven; and you will receive the gift of the Holy Spirit. For the promise is for you, for your children, and for all who are far away, everyone whom the Lord our God calls to him." . . . So those who welcomed his message were baptized,

and that day about three thousand persons were added. They devoted themselves to the apostles' teaching and fellowship, to the breaking of bread and the prayers. (Acts 2:38–42)

On this day the disciples' message about Jesus became the good news proclaimed by the church. The church was born by the power of the Spirit and was united in its central message and mission. We are called to be its embodiment today! It is fitting that we celebrate this special day with great significance. This is the one day on the liturgical calendar when the color of the paraments are to be red, representing the fire of the Holy Spirit. Encourage the wearing of red (or orange or yellow) by your congregation as well. This is a day to highlight the mission of the church and the calling of all the baptized to serve Christ in word and deed and to celebrate the gifts of the Spirit that equip the church for its mission in the world. Plan a full and rich service of worship for this significant day, including the Lord's Supper—and the sacrament of baptism if there are those to be baptized.

Questions for Reflection

1. What are some ways your congregation could extend the celebration of Easter beyond just one morning and into a whole season?
2. What activities or resources might help your congregants reflect on the meaning of Easter for their own baptismal identity and spiritual life?
3. Is Pentecost a memorable day in your congregation? What makes it special? How could you increase the day's significance?

Chapter Thirteen

Liturgical Odds and Ends: Meaningful Moments and Conversations

Having considered such centrally significant days and seasons as Advent, Christmas, Epiphany, Lent, Holy Week, Easter, and Pentecost, other days and other liturgical issues may seem to pale in comparison as just a collection of liturgical odds and ends. But there are other days and issues to consider, and they can be significant in their own way.

One issue is Ordinary Time. What is that? For one thing, it is more than half the Sundays of the year. Each Lord's Day is a day to worship God and to celebrate the presence of the living Christ in our midst. For this reason, every Sunday is special, even if some liturgical calendars designate it as being in Ordinary Time.

There are two extended periods of Ordinary Time. The shorter period begins after Christmas and Epiphany and concludes with the beginning of Lent. There is a much longer period of Ordinary Time that begins after Pentecost and continues through the summer and fall to the beginning of Advent. What is called Ordinary Time is a sequence of Sundays when there are no special liturgical days or seasons.

There are, however, special days both before and after each of the periods of Ordinary Time during the year that provide a sort of transition into and out of Ordinary Time. For instance, at the beginning of the shorter period of Ordinary Time, following Epiphany, there is a special Sunday called the Baptism of the Lord Sunday. This Sunday marks Jesus' baptism by John. The voice from heaven announces, "You are my Son, the Beloved; with you I am well pleased" (Mark 1:11). This is a day to remember both the baptism of Jesus and our own baptism and its meaning for us. At the end of this period of Ordinary Time, on the Sunday before Ash Wednesday, there is another special day called the Transfiguration of the Lord Sunday. The significance of the transfigured appearance of Jesus connects him to the revelation of God through the law (represented by Moses) and the prophets (represented by Elijah). The voice from heaven proclaims, "This is my Son, the Beloved; listen to him!" (Mark 9:7).

Additional special days occur in the second, longer period of Ordinary Time. At the beginning of this period is Trinity Sunday. This Sunday celebrates that God, incarnate in Jesus, is also present as the Holy Spirit. This is the mystery of the Trinity. Following many Sundays of Ordinary Time is another special Sunday called the Reign of Christ Sunday (also called Christ the King). This is a relatively recent observance, having been instituted in 1925 by Pope Pius XI, who warned of the threat posed by rising secular dictators in Europe. In 1934, in response to the absolutism of the Nazis and their racist agenda, delegates representing Lutheran, Reformed, and United churches met in the German town of Barmen-Wuppertal to declare that "Jesus Christ, as he is attested for us in Holy Scripture, is the one Word of God which we have to hear and which we have to trust and obey in life and in death."[1] Reformed theologian Karl Barth and Lutheran theologian and martyr Dietrich Bonhoeffer, among others, were Protestant leaders significantly involved in the Christian resistance to Hitler's movement. Fittingly, the liturgical year that began with the advent of Christ concludes with the reign of Christ, who is supremely God's Word to us.

Two other days should be mentioned: Reformation Sunday and All Saints' Day. The first of these commemorates the reformation of the medieval church that occurred in the sixteenth century. It is celebrated on the last Sunday of October by many Protestant denominations, especially Lutheran and Reformed traditions. It is a day to highlight the prophetic voices of the reformation—Martin Luther, John Calvin, and others—and to emphasize the central importance of the Word of God in Scripture and the affirmation of the priesthood of all believers.

All Saints' Day has a long and complicated history going back as far as 270 CE. Its purpose was to honor all saints and martyrs, not just those who were given a special day in the church's calendar. It is celebrated on November 1, which is most often a week day and only occasionally a Sunday. This presents an opportunity for a significant service of worship on a day other than Sunday. An All Saints' service appropriately includes the reading of the names of church members and those important to the congregation who have died in the past year. Perhaps a bell is tolled or a candle is lit as each name is read and remembered. All Saints' Day may also be celebrated on the following Sunday when a weekday service is not possible or practical. Remembering All Saints' Day in worship can be a positive experience for the children of the congregation who are influenced by Halloween to think of the dead only as frightening ghosts and not as beloved family and friends who are sadly missed and greatly loved.

Even with the festivals of the church year and all the special days scattered through Ordinary Time, what remains is still more than half the year. Ordinary Time serves to remind us that every Lord's Day is a special day because its central purpose is to celebrate the divine presence of the risen Christ in our midst. No special emphasis, liturgical or civic, should overshadow this central meaning of the Lord's Day. The designation of too many special Sundays for this and for that tends to obscure the fact that every Sunday is already special.

Given the length of the second period of Ordinary Time (summer and fall), many preachers find this period an ideal time to offer a preaching series. Such a series can incorporate one of the historic creeds of the church as a focus of preaching and instruction. Perhaps preaching through an entire book of the Bible would be edifying for a congregation. Perhaps addressing important theological or pastoral questions of significance for the congregation would be especially engaging. If Ordinary Time is about growth in Christian faith and discipleship, a lengthy season is a gift. We need time to grow.

This is the appropriate time to mention all the liturgical colors used to denote changing seasons and festivals of the liturgical year. Christmas and Easter are white to represent the central significance of the redemptive work of Christ. The color for the reflective/penitential seasons of Advent and Lent is traditionally purple, though some traditions use blue for Advent. Pentecost is red. The color for both periods of Ordinary Time is green, representing time for growth in the life of Christian faith and discipleship. The special days of Trinity Sunday, All Saints' Day, and the Reign of Christ, even though in Ordinary Time, are also white. Reformation Sunday, however, remains green.

Churches vary greatly in their use of the liturgical colors. Some do not use them at all. In others, worship leaders wear stoles in the liturgical colors. Many churches use colored paraments to hang from the pulpit and/or lectern and to cover the Communion table. Using the liturgical colors can alert the congregation to the changing seasons and days of the liturgical calendar and can be an avenue for teaching their theological meaning.

A final issue to mention in this chapter of odds and ends is the often-urgent conversation about traditional versus contemporary worship. What most needs to be remembered is that all Christian worship is by definition always *both* traditional and contemporary. Worship should be centered on the tradition of faith drawn from the historic life of the people of God and expressed in the Scriptures, and it should address the current conditions, needs, and challenges of a congregation in its contemporary context. Congregations are well advised to use different words to distinguish between these different worship services or styles.

The essential dynamics of worship should be the same, whether accompanied by guitar or piano or organ or

African drums and whether worshipers are dressed casually or formally or in between. Other matters are much more important for determining good worship. Does the order of worship make any sense, does it nourish us and push us toward discipleship and service in our daily lives, or is it just a random list of things to do? Is a full menu of Scripture passages read in the service? Is the preaching an exposition of the message of one or more of those Scripture passages? Is the message relevant, and does it connect with the experiences and needs of the congregation? Do the worshipers participate actively in the worship? Do they share regularly in joyful eucharistic celebrations of the Lord's Supper? Are the hymns and songs true to the message of the gospel? Do the worship services motivate worshipers to active discipleship? These are the kinds of questions that must be asked of all worship, whether it is called traditional or contemporary or blended or anything else.

Questions for Reflection

1. Which of the one-day celebrations mentioned in this chapter do you currently celebrate in your congregation? Which do you not currently celebrate? Why?

2. The first period of Ordinary Time begins and ends with the voice from heaven saying to Jesus, "You are my Son, the Beloved; with you I am well pleased. . . . Listen to him!" What significance does this hold for you?

3. The second period of Ordinary Time includes the long stretch of time from summer to fall. How might a preaching series for a portion of this time be helpful for a congregation?

Chapter Fourteen

Is Worship Important?

Having spent time in this book reflecting on worship in general, on the service of the Lord's Day in its historic form and flow, on the liturgical year experienced in a number of days and seasons, and on music and the arts in worship, we finally must ask, Is worship really all that important? For many, the answer is no. An increasingly large percentage of people today live their lives without organized congregational worship and without the church. Many of those who have been raised in the church do not return as adults, and many of their children are being brought up without any personal contact with a congregation. As Loren Mead has observed, what was once thought of as the mission field is now right outside the doors of the church.[1]

The complaint is often raised that churches are full of old, gray-haired people. There are indeed many gray-haired people in congregations, and many of them are amazing. Get to know them, and you will discover interesting people who have made all sorts of unique contributions to the lives of others, to the church, and to the world. This raises a different question: Why do so many people remain active in congregations into their graying years? Does church provide something valuable for a whole lifetime—a communion, a tradition, a true and abiding faith to live and practice? There seems to be plenty of evidence that this is the case.

The description of the church as just a bunch of old people, though, is plainly false. If you really become involved in a congregational community, you will begin to notice that there are actually people of all ages there, from babies to teenagers to young adults and beyond. In many congregations, those same graying believers are among those who are providing finances, personal interest, encouragement, and support for a small group of young people who are finding their way to a meaningful faith.

Of course, we must take seriously the problems, weaknesses, and deficiencies of the church in our time. We should take a good look at ourselves and become more aware of our own blind spots and the assumptions and habits that we so easily enshrine as eternal verities. But that does not mean we should give up on the church and join the loud chorus that criticizes it for not being as efficient as a corporation or as with it as a rock band. Rather, let us again catch a larger vision of the church as the body of Christ. As Simon Chan writes,

> The expression *body of Christ* is more than a metaphor for some intimate social dynamic between Christ and his church. It is an ontological reality, as Christ is ontologically real. Thus Lutheran theologian Anders Nygren could write, "The Church is Christ as he is present among us and meets us upon earth after his resurrection. . . . Christ is present in his Church through

his Word and sacrament, and the Church is, in its essence, nothing other than the presence of Christ."[2]

This picture of the church is a correction of the view that the church is just a voluntary organization for the improvement of society. This view sees the church as God's creation and God's work. Its life is not governed by business principles or human sociology but by the mission of God. As stated in the *Book of Order* of the Presbyterian Church (U.S.A.), "God has put all things under the Lordship of Jesus Christ and has made Christ Head of the Church, which is his body. The Church's life and mission are a joyful participation in Christ's ongoing life and work."[3]

As never before, we need to *be* the church and not just belong to the church. Being the church is more than a vague idea or ideal. Being the church is concretely expressed in consistent patterns of action (practices or virtues) that we engage in together. To be the church is to be formed by the church's tradition of a life of faith through things we do individually and together, such as immersing ourselves in the message and thought world of the Scriptures and participating in the sacramental life of the church. It is also expressed in engaging in corporate and individual prayer and meditation; being stewards of the resources of God and supporting the ministry of the whole church in a disciplined way; caring for one another through mutual concern and active support; responding to God's purpose through service to others; working for peace, justice, and freedom in the world; and sharing our faith in Christ with others through word and deed. Central to *all* Christian practices is worship in community with others.

The church is not just a human club, institution, or organization. It is a holy community, set apart for God's own purposes. It doesn't live or die by an up or down vote. It will survive all the caricatures of the media. The church lives by the grace of God. The church grows by giving itself away. It survives not by being hip but by being faithful. It is nourished by God through Word and sacrament. The church is important because it is the expression of God's mission through Christ leading us to God's new day.

All the practices and actions we have just mentioned are important because the church is important. Worship is especially important because it is not just one of these practices, but it is the central and formative practice that shapes and sustains all the others. In worship, everything comes together in one way or another. In worship, we are called to be in one place together, both physically and spiritually. In worship, we think about and pray about and celebrate what God is calling us to be and do.

Worship is the church's essential and primary spiritual practice. It is not just an expected churchly routine. It is not just one church program among others. It is not entertainment that we expect to amuse us. Done poorly or done wonderfully, it is the real deal. But by all means, let us strive to do worship as wonderfully, effectively, and sensitively as we possibly can. Let it not be dulled by routine or taken for granted. Let everything be carefully planned. Inform and rehearse participants who will take some part in leading the service. Be prepared for the unexpected, and leave as little as possible to chance. Be prepared to be in awe, for this is an encounter with the living God. When you are done, find a time to meet together, as planners and participants, to discuss together what worked and what didn't, what you might learn from the experience, and what you should change the next time you meet for worship. Most importantly, share with one another how worship has shaped and formed you as a person of Christian faith and as a disciple of Jesus Christ. After all is said and done, it is very clear: worship matters.

Questions for Reflection

1. "Worship is the church's essential and primary spiritual practice." Do you agree or disagree? Why?
2. It has been widely observed that the mainline church is in decline. How might vibrant and engaging worship offer us a more hopeful future?
3. What has been the most thought-provoking chapter of this book for you? Why?

Notes

1. The Order—Not Just a Grocery List

1. Referred to in liturgical literature as the *ordo*. For further reading, see Alexander Schmemann, *Introduction to Liturgical Theology* (Crestwood, NY: St. Vladimir's Seminary Press, 1986), chap. 1, and Gordon Lathrop, *Holy Things* (Minneapolis: Fortress Press, 1993), 33.

2. The Gathering

1. Gordon Lathrop, *Holy Things* (Minneapolis: Fortress Press, 1993), 87.
2. Glory be to the Father,
   and to the Son,
   and to the Holy Ghost;
   as it was in the beginning,
   is now,
   and ever shall be,
   world without end. Amen.
3. Glory to God in the highest,
   and peace to God's people on earth.
   Lord God, heavenly King,
   almighty God and Father,
   we worship you, we give you thanks,
   we praise you for your glory.
   Lord Jesus Christ, only Son of the Father,

Lord God, Lamb of God,
you take away the sin of the world:
have mercy upon us;
you are seated at the right hand of the Father:
receive our prayer.
For you alone are the Holy One,
you alone are the Lord,
you alone are the Most High,
Jesus Christ,
with the Holy Spirit,
in the glory of God the Father. Amen.

3. Addressed by the Word

1. The Revised Common Lectionary (1992), created by the Consultation on Common Texts, is widely used by many parts of the ecumenical church.

4. The Joyful Feast

1. *Book of Common Worship* (Louisville, KY: Westminster John Knox Press, 1993), 68.
2. Ibid, 42.
3. *The Service for the Lord's Day*, Supplemental Liturgical Resource 1, (Philadelphia: Westminster Press, 1984).

5. Sent to Serve

1. *Book of Common Worship* (Louisville, KY: Westminster John Knox Press, 1993), 44–45.
2. See J. C. Hoekendijk, *The Church Inside Out*, trans. I. C. Rottenberg (Philadelphia: Westminster Press, 1966).
3. *Book of Common Worship*, 78.

6. Music and the Arts in Worship

1. Thomas Long, *Beyond the Worship Wars* (Bethesda, MD: Alban Institute, 2001), 60.

7. Worship for Special Times

1. *Liturgical Year*, Supplemental Liturgical Resource 7 (Louisville, KY: Westminster John Knox Press, 1992), 21.

8. Celebrating Christmas (and Epiphany)

1. John Polkinghorne, *Living with Hope* (Louisville, KY: Westminster John Knox Press, 2003), 71.
2. Ibid, 70.

10. Celebrating Easter

1. Alexander Schmemann, *Of Water and the Spirit: A Liturgical Study of Baptism* (Crestwood, NY: St. Vladimir's Seminary Press, 1974), 7.
2. More information is available from www.catechumenate.org.
3. Aidan Kavanagh, *The Shape of Baptism: The Rite of Christian Initiation* (New York: Pueblo Publishing Co., 1978), 5.

11. Lent and Holy Week: Journeying with Christ

1. From the Heidelberg Catechism of 1562 in *The Constitution of the Presbyterian Church (U.S.A.)*, Part I, *Book of Confessions* (Louisville, KY: Office of the General Assembly, Presbyterian Church (U.S.A.), 2007), 4.001.

13. Liturgical Odds and Ends: Meaningful Moments and Conversations

1. From the Theological Declaration of Barmen in *The Constitution of the Presbyterian Church (U.S.A.)*, Part I, *Book of Confessions* (Louisville, KY: Office of the General Assembly, Presbyterian Church (U.S.A.), 2007), 8.11.

14. Is Worship Important?

1. For further reading, see Loren B. Mead, *The Once and Future Church* (Washington, DC: Alban Institute, 1991).
2. Simon Chan, *Liturgical Theology: The Church as Worshiping Community* (Downers Grove, IL: IVP Academic, 2006), 27.
3. *The Constitution of the Presbyterian Church (U.S.A.)*, Part II, *Book of Order* (Louisville, KY: Office of the General Assembly, Presbyterian Church (U.S.A.), 2013), F-1.0201.

Bibliography

Book of Common Worship. Louisville, KY: Westminster John Knox Press, 1993.

Chan, Simon. *Liturgical Theology: The Church as Worshiping Community.* Downers Grove, IL: IVP Academic, 2006.

The Constitution of the Presbyterian Church (U.S.A.). Part I, *Book of Confessions.* Louisville, KY: Office of the General Assembly, Presbyterian Church (U.S.A.), 2007.

———. Part II, *The Book of Order.* Louisville, KY: Office of the General Assembly, Presbyterian Church (U.S.A.), 2013.

Hoekendijk, J. C. *The Church Inside Out.* Translated by I. C. Rottenberg. Philadelphia: Westminster Press, 1966.

Kavanagh, Aidan. *The Shape of Baptism: The Rite of Christian Initiation.* New York: Pueblo Publishing Co., 1978.

Lathrop, Gordon, *Holy Things.* Minneapolis: Fortress Press, 1993.

Long, Thomas, *Beyond the Worship Wars.* Bethesda, MD: Alban Institute, 2001.

Mead, Loren B. *The Once and Future Church.* Washington, DC: Alban Institute, 1991.

Polkinghorne, John. *Living with Hope.* Louisville, KY: Westminster John Knox Press, 2003.

Presbyterian Church (U.S.A.). *The Service for the Lord's Day*, Supplemental Liturgical Resource 1. Philadelphia: Westminster Press, 1984.

———. *Liturgical Year*, Supplemental Liturgical Resource 7. Louisville, KY: Westminster/John Knox Press, 1992.

Schmemann, Alexander. *Introduction to Liturgical Theology*. Crestwood,
NY: St. Vladimir's Seminary Press, 1986.

———. *Of Water and the Spirit: A Liturgical Study of Baptism*. Crestwood, NY: St. Vladimir's Seminary Press, 1974.

264
S8448 LINCOLN CHRISTIAN UNIVERSITY

130190